moment
meditations

A CUP of GOD'S LOVE

Emilie Barnes

Harvest House Publishers
Eugene, Oregon

To Annabel...
With ♡
Barb Shaw
September 26, 1995

W9-DAU-176

A Cup of God's Love
Copyright ©1999 Harvest House Publishers
Eugene, Oregon 97402

ISBN 0-7369-0030-6

Text is adapted from *Fill My Cup, Lord*, by Emilie Barnes
(Harvest House Publishers, 1996).

Design and production by Left Coast Design, Portland, Oregon.
Artwork by Gwen Babbitt

Printed in China

99 00 01 02 03 04 05 06 07 08 / PP / 10 9 8 7 6 5 4 3 2 1

ill my cup, Lord." I hope that's your heartcry, too, as you open this book. Come to him as you are, cup in hand, and hold it up to receive the Lord's outpouring of comfort, strength, and everlasting peace. And then you will say, with wonder and amazement as your life overflows with his blessings, "Surely…my cup runneth over."

It's such a simple, beautiful process. We hold up our cup to our loving, giving heavenly Father. He cleanses us of the old, the impure, the bitter. Then he fills our cup with living water—fills it with quietness, with encouragement and forgiveness, with trust and communion, strength and thanksgiving.

You must be emptied of that which fills you, that you may be filled with that of which you are empty.

ADAPTED FROM AUGUSTINE

*Whoever drinks the water
I give him will never thirst.*

JOHN 4:14 NIV

Gwendolyn
Babbitt

Your quiet time is not a gift you give to God. Your quiet time is a gift God gives to you. Don't offer him your quiet time. Simply offer him your time, your self. He's the one who provides the quiet spirit.

He restores my soul.

PSALM 23:3

*I*f you offer to God whatever time you have, he honors that time. The sweet taste of his peace will leave you wanting more and more.

Whatever is your best time in the day, give that to communion with God.

HUDSON TAYLOR

Chris Cupboard 2-5-98

You will keep him in perfect peace, whose mind is stayed on You, because he trusts You.

ISAIAH 26:3

Those who wait on the Lord shall renew their strength.

ISAIAH 40:31

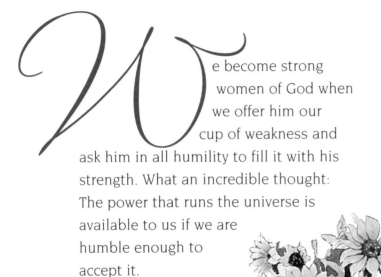

We become strong women of God when we offer him our cup of weakness and ask him in all humility to fill it with his strength. What an incredible thought: The power that runs the universe is available to us if we are humble enough to accept it.

The Lord doesn't ask about your ability, only your availability, and, if you prove your dependability, the Lord will increase your capability.

SOURCE UNKNOWN

Focusing on the positive doesn't mean being naive or unrealistic or blind. It simply means learning to accept yourself and others for what you are—human beings with faults and good points and also the capacity to grow.

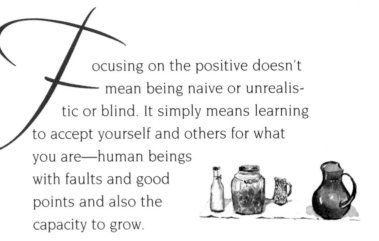

Accepting one's life means also accepting the sin of others which causes us suffering, accepting their nerves, their reactions, their enthusiasms, and even the talents and qualities by means of which they outshine us.

PAUL TOURNIER

Encourage the timid, help the weak, be patient with everyone.

1 THESSALONIANS 5:14 NIV

Give unto the LORD the glory due unto his name: bring an offering, and come before him: worship the LORD in the beauty of holiness.

1 CHRONICLES 16:29 KJV

Like the colors of a watercolor painting, forgiving and being forgiven run together, creating surprising and unforgettable patterns. Forgiveness is a gift of God.

God pardons like a mother,
who kisses the offense into
everlasting forgiveness.

HENRY WARD BEECHER

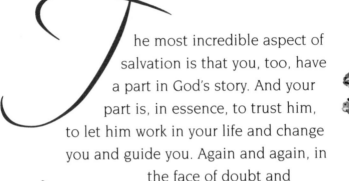

*T*he most incredible aspect of salvation is that you, too, have a part in God's story. And your part is, in essence, to trust him, to let him work in your life and change you and guide you. Again and again, in the face of doubt and despair, God will prove himself trustworthy.

Build a little fence of trust today; fill the space with loving deeds, and therein stay. Look not through the sheltering bars upon tomorrow; God will help thee bear what comes of joy and sorrow.

MARY F. BUTTS

*Trust in the LORD, and do good; dwell
in the land, and feed on His faithfulness.*

PSALM 37:3

f we are depending on God, we move closer to that beautiful picture he wants to paint in the world through us. We move closer to him, and we learn to follow him better.

I tell you the truth, anyone who has faith in me will do what I have been doing. He will do even greater things than these, because I am going to the Father.

JOHN 14:12 NIV

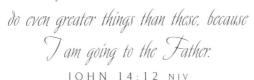

There's more to living in the Lord's strength than just "soaking" in Scripture and prayer. The actual process of becoming strong and beautiful takes a bit more energy. It's a matter of doing what we think God wants us to do, trusting that we will be given the strength we need when we need it.

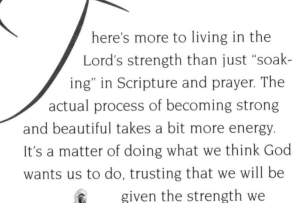

There is only one way to bring peace to the heart, joy to the mind, and beauty to the life; it is to accept and do the will of God.

WILLIAM BARCLAY

Look to the LORD and his strength; seek his face always.

PSALM 105:4 NIV

Thanks be to God, who always leads us in triumphal procession in Christ.

2 CORINTHIANS 2:14 NIV

An attitude of thankfulness is a gift God gives to us, a healing libation he pours into our cups. But we must choose to accept it, even to ask for it. Our part is to offer whatever is in our cup to the Lord, and then ask him to fill our cup with true thankfulness.

To speak gratitude is courteous and pleasant, to enact gratitude is generous and noble, but to live gratitude is to touch heaven.

JOHANNES A. GAERTNER

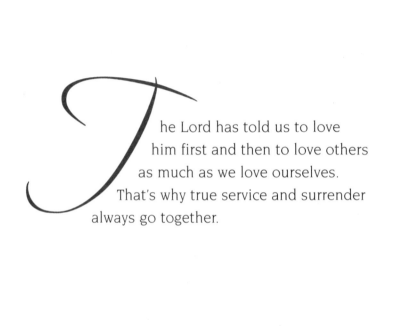

The Lord has told us to love him first and then to love others as much as we love ourselves. That's why true service and surrender always go together.

If anyone
serves, he should
do it with the strength
God provides, so that
in all things God may be praised through Jesus Christ.
1 PETER 4:11 NIV

Restore to me the joy of Your salvation, and uphold me with Your generous Spirit.

PSALM 51:12

*W*ash out your cup, and then get it refilled from God's bubbling bounty. Keep your cup filled with love and acceptance and affirmation and encouragement from a dependable Source.

In confession...we open our lives to the healing, reconciling, restoring, uplifting grace of him who loves us in spite of what we are.

LOUIS CASSELS

*Q*uiet times can happen anywhere, as long as you are able to pull away, to shut a door, to put space between you and the ordinary demands of your day.

God has not bowed to our nervous haste nor embraced the methods of our machine age. The man who would know God must give time to Him.

A. W. Tozer

Come to Me, all you who labor and are heavy laden, and I will give you rest. Take My yoke upon you and learn from Me, for I am gentle and lowly in heart, and you will find rest for your souls.

MATTHEW 11:28

If you return to the Almighty, you will be restored.

JOB 22:23 NIV

The Lord is always there for you, waiting to fill your cup with encouragement and affirmation, waiting mercifully to restore your soul. He does it through the words of Scripture, through the soft whisper of his Holy Spirit, and especially through the people who love and accept and support you.

An infinite God can give all of Himself to each of His children.

WILLIAM WARD

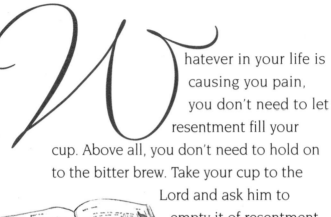

*W*hatever in your life is causing you pain, you don't need to let resentment fill your cup. Above all, you don't need to hold on to the bitter brew. Take your cup to the Lord and ask him to empty it of resentment and guilt, to fill it with sparkling forgiveness.

If you hug to yourself any resentment against anybody else, you destroy the bridge by which God would come to you.

PETER MARSHALL

Create in me a clean heart, O God, And renew a steadfast spirit within me.

PSALM 51:10

© Gwendolyn Babbitt

*R*eal trust is a gift you give to someone you love. It's a compliment, a gesture of respect. And it's also a way of helping them grow, to become more trustworthy.

Whoever can be trusted with very little can also be trusted with much.

LUKE 16:10 NIV

The Lord asks for the whole of your life. Sometimes it feels like a blessed relief, sometimes a painful sacrifice, often a mixture of the two. You give him all you can of yourself. He fills you with all you could ever want of him. And then he gives you back yourself as well.

Gratitude is not only the memory but the homage of the heart rendered to God for His goodness.

NATHANIEL P. WILLIS

*Love the LORD your God with all your heart
and with all your soul and with all your strength.*

DEUTERONOMY 6:5 NIV

I pray also for those who will believe in me
through their message, that all of them may be one.

JOHN 17:20,21 NIV

Communion is what happens whenever spirits are shared and cups are filled with love. It's what happens whenever human beings draw near to each other and to God, managing somehow to emerge from their separateness and partake of the shared life God intended.

In His will is our peace.

DANTE

God doesn't expect us to be strong, just obedient. We have to follow up on the little nudges and the big messages he has sent us in our quiet times. We have to step forward, trusting that the Lord who gave the orders will also provide the strength to carry them out.

For the eyes of the LORD range throughout the earth to strengthen those whose hearts are fully committed to him.

2 CHRONICLES 16:9 NIV

In this you greatly rejoice, though now for a little while, if need be, you have been grieved by various trials, that the genuineness of your faith . . . may be found to praise, honor, and glory at the revelation of Jesus Christ, whom having not seen you love.

1 PETER 1:6, 7

To fill our cup with thanksgiving
means to live in the belief that
God is working for good even
when things seem
to be falling apart.

Gratitude is not only the greatest of
virtues, but the parent of all the others.

CICERO

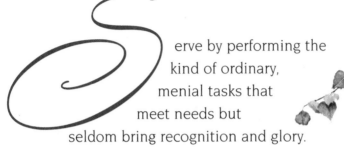

*S*erve by performing the kind of ordinary, menial tasks that meet needs but seldom bring recognition and glory. Any humble chore, when done in Jesus' name, can be a graceful dance of love.

In the service of the Lord, it is not where but how you serve.

J. REUBEN CLARK

*I was hungry and you gave Me food; I was thirsty and
you gave Me drink; I was a stranger and you took
Me in; I was naked and you clothed Me.*

MATTHEW 25:35,36

Gwendo[...]
Babbit[...]

ill my cup with your love, Lord.
Help me to feel your hands
holding mine, feel your
arms around me, feel your
love empowering
me. Fill me with
quietness and
encouragement
and trust.

*Therefore I tell you, whatever
you ask for in prayer, believe that you
have received it, and it will be yours.*

MARK 11:24 NIV

If you will just hold up your cup to him, even a cup of anger and stress and trouble and confusion, he will be faithful to fill your cup with the peace of his presence.

Peace I leave with you, My peace I give to you; not as the world gives do I give to you. Let not your heart be troubled, neither let it be afraid.

JOHN 14:27

Gwen
Babbitt

Chris' Cupboard 2-5-98

We are children of God, created by him. He made us each beautiful in his sight. Make the effort to find that beauty in yourself and others.

Above all things have fervent love for one another, for "love will cover a multitude of sins."

I PETER 4:8

orgiveness of others works at the soul level, and that is why forgiveness often doesn't seem to change anything—at least not right away. True forgiveness works because it changes you. But that, of course, changes everything.

Humanity is never so beautiful as when praying for forgiveness or else forgiving another.

JEAN PAUL RICHTER

Commit your way to the LORD, trust also in Him, and He shall bring it to pass. He shall bring forth your righteousness as the light, and your justice as the noonday.

PSALM 37:5,6

The LORD is my strength and my shield; my heart trusted in Him, and I am helped; therefore my heart greatly rejoices, and with my song I will praise Him.

PSALM 28:7

The more you trust God, the more you'll come to know his character, and to stare in amazement at what he's done in your life and wait in anticipation for what he's going to do next.

God is the sunshine that warms us, the rain that melts the frost and waters the young plants. The presence of God is a climate of strong and bracing love, always there.

JOAN ARNOLD

The cup of communion is a gift from creation, part of how we are made. God created us to connect to each other. He made us with the need for other people and the desire to live in harmony.

Finally, all of you, live in harmony with one another; be sympathetic, love as brothers, be compassionate and humble.

1 PETER 3:8 NIV

We do not have a High Priest who cannot sympathize with our weaknesses. . . . Let us therefore come boldly to the throne of grace, that we may obtain mercy and find grace to help in time of need.

HEBREWS 4:15,16

*O*ur Lord is no stranger to pain. He chose to become human, to share our pain in order to move us beyond it. Our Lord is with us in our pain, but he also is greater than pain, greater than fear, greater even than death.

God brings men into deep waters not to drown them, but to cleanse them.

JOHN H. ANGEY

Lord, for *whatever* I am receiving and about to receive—pain as well as joy— please teach me the secret of giving thanks. For what I have already received—what has shaped my life in the past, and what is shaping me today—please fill my cup with thankfulness.

Gratitude bestows reverence, allowing us to encounter everyday epiphanies, those transcendent moments of awe that change forever how we experience life and the world.

JOHN MILTON

Give thanks in all circumstances, for this is God's will for you in Christ Jesus.

1 THESSALONIANS
5:18 NIV

*P*rayer can be a form of service in itself, but it also increases our capacity and desire to serve in other ways. When we are coming to the Lord regularly in prayer, we are usually growing in compassion, growing in understanding, growing in our willingness to serve.

Our hope is that, as your faith continues to grow, our area of activity among you will greatly expand, so that we can preach the gospel in the regions beyond you.

2 CORINTHIANS 10:15,16 NIV

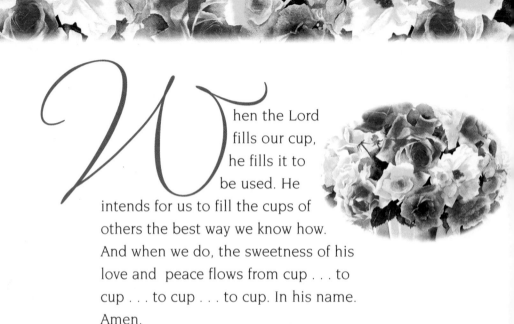

When the Lord fills our cup, he fills it to be used. He intends for us to fill the cups of others the best way we know how. And when we do, the sweetness of his love and peace flows from cup . . . to cup . . . to cup . . . to cup. In his name. Amen.

Walk in love, as Christ also has loved us and given Himself for us, an offering and a sacrifice to God.

EPHESIANS 5:2